NATIONAL
GEOGRAPHIC

T0061064

Drop by Drop

PIONEER EDITION

By Daphne Liu and Jim Enote

CONTENTS

Jonathan Waterman walks on the dry bed of the Colorado River, ten miles from the Gulf of California.

© PETE MCBRIDE

TROUBLED WATERS

Its powerful waters carved the Grand Canyon. Now the mighty Colorado River is drying up. Ride downstream to follow the twists and turns of this American river.

BY DAPHNE LIU

Jonathan Waterman was hot. Dirt crunched under his feet. He wasn't in a desert. He was standing in the Colorado River, near Mexico. Once, there was rushing water where he walked. Now it was gone.

Waterman was disappointed. He had wanted to paddle down the river, from beginning to end. He started on a raft at one of the river's sources in the Rocky Mountains. Now he was carrying his raft.

Water Worries

As Waterman walked, he worried about the river. People in the American West depend on it. Yet it might not be there in the future. Worse yet, people are causing the problems. They block the river's path. Pipes carry its water to far-off places. Farmers use its water to grow crops.

The Headwaters

Waterman's adventure began in the mountains in Colorado. He put his raft into a stream of melted snow that runs down the mountain slopes. The icy stream flows into others, forming the mighty river.

Waterman paddled on. He crossed into Utah. The river kept changing. In some places, he paddled through slow moving water that cut through deep canyons. In other places, the river tossed Waterman's raft against rocks that formed rapids.

The Colorado River runs 2,333 kilometers (1,450 miles). In places, travelers cross white-water rapids (below).

Water Power

Weeks later, he neared the border with Arizona. That's where he saw Glen Canyon **Dam**. The dam is a huge wall that blocks the river. It holds back most of the water, but lets some through. This forms a huge lake. People get drinking water from the lake. They also swim in the lake.

People also get electricity from the dam and river. River water rushes through huge machines inside the dam. The water turns blades in the machines. The moving blades create electricity. The electricity is used in homes, schools, and businesses. This is called **hydroelectric power**.

This is the Glen Canyon Dam in Arizona. More than a dozen dams slow the flow of the river.

At Horseshoe Bend, the river carved a deep curve through rock.

Crossing the Canyon

Soon, Waterman paddled into the Grand Canyon. It took millions of years for the river to carve the canyon. It cut through solid rock to make the canyon.

The canyon walls are steep and high. They are layered with colored rock called strata.

Each layer comes from a different time in Earth's history. Waterman now thought of his raft as a time machine. The deeper into the canyon he went, the further back in time he went. You see, the oldest rocks are at the bottom of the canyon.

Large Lake

Waterman came out of the canyon as he neared Nevada. Here the Hoover Dam blocks the river. It weighs more than 800,000 African elephants.

The dam forms a large lake. People get water and electricity from this lake and dam, too. But the river on the other side of the dam is much smaller than it used to be.

Water Problems

In all, fourteen dams block different parts of the Colorado River. The dams have changed the river. They also have changed ecosystems.

For example, the river used to carry **silt**. Silt is made up of bits of soil, sand, and rock. Silt is important. It gives nutrients to plants and animals living along the river. Today, much of the silt is gone. It is trapped behind the dams.

Climate change affects the river, too. As Earth warms, less snow falls in the mountains. That means less water in the river. Without silt and water from lots of melting snow, fewer plants and animals live along and in the river.

Waterman did see signs of hope. People are planting trees and protecting wildlife. They are also talking about ways to better use the water so that the dams don't block as much of it. One day, parts of the river may run as wild as they did when the Grand Canyon formed.

WORDWISE

dam: concrete wall that blocks the flow of a river

hydroelectric power: electricity produced by the force of moving water

silt: bits of soil, sand and rock

© JOE MCDONALD/CORBIS

ringtail cat

Here, the river flows between the steep, colorful walls of the Grand Canyon.

Sunlight turns the river green at Emerald Cave in Arizona.

At night Waterman camps under the stars, thinking of the river's twists and turns.

Water Source. *Water is scarce in the Southwest. People there have learned how to use it wisely.*

The Wonder of Water

Living in a dry place, some Native Americans know
what everyone needs to remember.
Water is precious.

By Jim Enote
Director, A:shiwi A:wan Museum and Heritage Center

When I was a boy, I spent a lot of time with my grandparents. My family belongs to the Zuni people. We are Native Americans from the Southwest. Summers there are hot and very dry.

Each day, my grandfather and I walked to a **spring** with clean, cold water. We needed that water to live.

"Water is precious," Grandma often said. "Always respect it." She showed her respect in art. She painted things having to do with water on clay bowls.

What's a Watershed?

The water in our spring comes from under the ground. If it became polluted, people would get sick.

When you think about water, you should think of whole **watersheds**. A watershed is all the land around a river, lake, or other body of water.

For example, melting snow may flow down a hill into a stream. The stream then flows into a river. If one spot becomes polluted, the pollution spreads to the rest of the watershed.

Everyone Wants Water

Pollution isn't the only challenge. Sharing is tough, too. If people in one area use too much water, people in other places won't have enough.

The demand for water is growing. That's because Earth has more people than ever before. In the future, we could have water **shortages**. A shortage is a lack of something.

Using Water Wisely

For my people, the need to **conserve**, or save, water is not new. I teach this message to young people.

I work with kids at a museum in New Mexico. They paint pictures showing what water means to them. I tell them the ways our people always used water wisely in the past.

I also teach kids a great way to grow things. We make gardens with big squares. Small, dirt walls go around each square. We grow plants in the squares. The walls keep water from flowing away. This way, no water is wasted.

© MARILYN ANGEL WYNN/NATIVESTOCK.COM

JESSE NUSBAUM, COURTESY PALACE OF THE GOVERNORS PHOTO ARCHIVES (NMHM/DCA), #87-40

Saving Water. *The Zuni's special gardens help them grow food without using too much water.*

When It Rains. *On this Zuni pot, frogs, butterflies, and water snakes represent the rain that falls in different seasons of the year.*

JENNIE LAATE, ZUNI PUEBLO, JAR, 1983; FROM THE COLLECTION OF THE HEARD MUSEUM, PHOENIX, ARIZONA

Zuni Landmark. *Springs near Corn Mountain make it important for the Zuni people.*

Wordwise

conserve: to use without wasting

shortage: lack of something

spring: place where water flows from the ground

watershed: land surrounding a river, lake, sea, or other body of water

What You Can Do

You can help save water, too. Think of all the ways you use water in a day. Are there ways you can use less water and still do the same things?

Turn off the water while you brush your teeth. Try taking shorter showers. Make it a family challenge! See who can get clean in the fastest time. Ask your family not to run the washing machine unless it is full.

These are simple steps, I know. Still, they can make a difference. Saving water will show you've learned a key lesson. It's the one my grandmother taught me: "Water is precious."

Rafting the River

Students at Georgia Avenue Elementary in Tennessee learned about watersheds. Thanks to the Wolf River Conservancy, they rafted on the Wolf River. This river flows into the Mississippi River. Students saw how living things need a watershed to survive.

Fifth grader Corina Brown saw cool critters and lots of trees. Seeing all these things taught Corina that "it's important to take care of nature."

Classmate Steven Mitchell agrees. He learned that a good way of keeping animals safe is to "keep water clean by not littering."

Water Is Precious

What did you learn about the importance of water? Answer these questions to find out.

 1. Name two ways people use the Colorado River.

 2. What do people need to do to take care of the Colorado River?

 3. What important lesson did Jim Enote learn from his grandmother?

 4. What are some ways to use water wisely?

 5. What ideas do Jonathan Waterman and Jim Enote share?

© KSBELL/SHUTTERSTOCK